Living the Good Life

Living the Good Life

by
Columbus O'Banner Jr.

www.hispubg.com
A division of HISpecialists, llc

Copyright © 2012 by Columbus O'Banner Jr
All rights reserved. No portion of this book may be reproduced or utilized in any form or by any means, electronic or mechanical including photocopying, recording or any information storage or retrieval systems without permission in writing from both the copyright owner and the publisher.
Inquiries should be addressed to
HIS Publishing Group, PO Box 12516, Dallas, Texas 75225.

Published by HIS Publishing Group,
a Division of Human Improvement Specialists, llc
Contact: info@hispubg.com

Scripture quotations taken from the Amplified® Bible,
Copyright © 1954, 1958, 1962, 1964, 1965, 1987
by The Lockman Foundation (www.lockman.org)
Used by permission.

Scriptures taken from *GOD'S WORD*.
Copyright 1995 God's Word to the Nations.
Used by permission of Baker Publishing Group. All rights reserved.

Scripture taken from *The Message*. Copyright © 1993, 1994, 1995, 1996, 2000, 2001, 2002. Used by permission of NavPress Publishing Group.

ISBN: 978-0-578-11630-3

Printed and bound in the United States of America

Dedication

I would like to dedicate my first book to the following people...

To my two grandmothers who are in heaven among the cloud of witnesses, Rachel O'Banner and Eliza Hooker. These two women had a direct influence upon me receiving Jesus as my Lord and Savior and my being filled with the Holy Spirit.

To my parents Columbus O'Banner Sr. & Flora Mae O'Banner who raised their children up in the church and taught us the Word of God!

To my wife Barbara O'Banner who loves the Lord and has supported me and stood by my side. To our children, Marquis L O'Banner and his wife DeMarias, Alisha Chandler and her husband Mario, Joycelyn D. O'Banner, and Victoria H. O'Banner. To our six grandchildren Elijah, Elyse, Caleb, Daysean, Dajah, and Kaiden.

To my Pastor, Joel Sims, Senior Pastor of Word of Life Church in Flowood, Mississippi and to my Mt. Moriah Church Family and my Columbus O'Banner Ministry Partners.

Table of Contents

Introduction 1

Chapter One
What is the *Good Life?* 5

Chapter Two
Why are some Christians not living the *Good Life?* 11

Chapter Three
Unforgiveness is a major hindrance
to the *Good Life* 19

Chapter Four
Rejecting God's knowledge will cause
destruction in your life 23

Chapter Five
Don't let your past keep you from the *Good Life* 27

Chapter Six
To live the *Good Life* you must renew your mind 33

Chapter Seven
God's Blessing and Favor Empowers You
To Be Successful 37

Chapter Eight
It is our time to shine 41

Prayer of Salvation 49
About the Author 51

~: Living the Good Life :~

Introduction

> ...*living the good life which He prearranged
> and made ready for us to live.*
> Ephesians 2.10

GOD HAS A WONDERFUL PLAN for His children; it is called the *good life*. It is not the will of God for the human race to be disconnected from Him. God is not willing for any person to perish, but that all people would come to repentance. It is not the will of God for His Children to be living a life of defeat or failure. God's will for His Children is to live a life of victory.

When satan, the enemy, brings sickness, poverty, lack, confusion, depression, or division in the life of an individual, God gets no glory out of those attacks upon your life. This is an attempt by satan to destroy your relationship and fellowship with God. The thief comes only to steal, to kill, and to bring destruction in the life of the people that were created by God.

However, we praise God that the enemy's weapons have been defeated over 2000 years ago by Jesus Christ. Jesus came that we may have abundant life. In Jesus, we have a better life, the *good life* that God prearranged for His children to live.

I will share a number of Bible verses in this book because it is very important to know what the Word of God has to say about our life. I could share some of my own experiences, but we all have different situation that we encounter in life. In saying that, we need to go back to the instructor's Manuel for life, the B-I-B-L-E (Basic Instruction Before Leaving Earth). There is no magical formal for success. The Word of God holds all the keys to a *good life* before God and the human race.

> For we are God's [own] handiwork (His workmanship), recreated in Christ Jesus, [born anew] that we may do those good works which God predestined (planned beforehand) for us [taking paths which He prepared ahead of time], that we should walk in them [living the *good life* which He prearranged and made ready for us to live].
> (Ephesians 2:10 AMP)

Are you living the *good life* that God has prearranged for you? Remember, this is the plan of God without your involvement before you were ever born.

> This Book of the Law shall not depart out of your mouth, but you shall meditate on it day and night, that you may observe and do according to all that is written in it. For then you shall make your way prosperous, and then you shall deal wisely and have good success.
> (Joshua 1:8 AMP)

Look at God's plan for success or living the *good life*: keep the word in your mouth, think about it day and night, observe or look at the Word, and do according to what is written in the book. In other words, follow the instructions.

> The thief cometh not, but for to steal, and to kill, and to destroy: I am come that they might have life, and that they might have it more abundantly.
> (JOHN 10:10 KJV)

Jesus came for us to live this life more abundantly!

In order for us to grasp the full understanding of what Jesus is offering, let us first look at the meaning of the word *life* from the Greek noun *Zoe* and then the meaning of the word *abundantly* from the Greek adjective *Perissos*.

Life derived from the Greek noun *Zoe*. (a) The absolute fullness of life, both essential and ethical, which belongs to God, and though him both to the hypo static "logos" and to Christ in whom the "logos" put on human nature and (b) life, real and genuine, a life active and vigorous, devoted to God, blessed, in the portion even in this world of those who put their trust in Christ, but after the resurrection to be consummated by new accessions (among them a more perfect body), and to last forever.

Abundant derived from the Greek adjective *Perissos*. Is in the sense of beyond; super abundant (in quantity) or superior (in quality); by implication, excessive; preeminence—exceeding abundantly above, more abundantly, advantage, exceedingly, very highly, beyond measure, more, superfluous, vehemently! Exceeding some number or measure or rank or need over and above, more than is necessary, superadded exceeding abundantly, supremely something further, more, much more than all, more plainly, superior, extraordinary, surpassing, uncommon, pre-eminence, superiority, advantage, more eminent, more remarkable, more excellent.

Praise God for the abundant life in Jesus, life that gives His children the advantage beyond measure!

> No weapon that is formed against thee shall prosper; and every tongue that shall rise against thee in judgment thou shalt condemn. This is the heritage of the servants of the Lord, and their righteousness is of me, saith the Lord.
> (ISAIAH 54:17 KJV)

No weapon formed against you will be successful. That means that any attack that the devil brings your way will fail against you. It could be an attack on your health, your wealth, your marriage, your relationship with your children, your job, or your assignment in life. Your final outcome will be good. You win!

> For I know the thoughts and plans that I have for you, says the Lord, thoughts and plans for welfare and peace and not for evil, to give you hope in your final outcome.
> (JEREMIAH 29:11 AMP)

Look at God's thoughts and plans for you, plans to prosper you, plans for peace throughout your life, and plans for hope for all people even if you have experienced failure in the pass. A quitter never wins, and a winner never quits. Just because you get knocked down doesn't mean you get knocked out of the *good life* God has for you. Your Father God is the Judge.

~: Chapter One :~

What Is the Good Life?

*…My counsel shall stand,
and I will do all my pleasure.
Isaiah 46:10 KJV*

THE GOOD LIFE IS THE LIFE that God has prearranged for His family to live! The plan that God has for us is that there would be nothing missing and nothing broken in our life. With our lives being complete in Christ, our lives are destined to be successful.

The Bible says that God declares the end in the beginning. Although God has prearranged this wonderful life for us, we still have to choose to receive it. The mistake that so many of us make is making choices without communicating with God in prayer. Thus, many of God's children never live for the purpose He created them to live.

I remember in my own life that at one time I lived in foolishness and sin. During that time, because I made choices that did not honor God, my life was a life filled with disappointment and confusion. Life was a real struggle before I receive Jesus into my Life.

I can remember growing up in church and doing some things that were right, but on the other hand, I did some things that were not right. I was living a life apart from a relationship with God the Father through God the Son, the Lord Jesus Christ.

Even when I first received God's plan of salvation in my life, I did not know about this *good life*. I knew that I was saved, but life still seemed difficult in certain areas because of my lack of knowledge about the will of God for my life. Once I started to get more knowledge about the will of God for my life, things begin to change.

As I began to trust in the Lord with all of my heart, my pathway in this life became enlightened to the *good life* the Lord had for me on the earth as well as an eternal life in heaven after my purpose on the earth is complete!

> Declaring the end from the beginning, and from ancient times the things that are not yet done, saying, My counsel shall stand, and I will do all my pleasure.
> (Isaiah 46:10 KJV)

Your life has already been seen and recorded completely by God before you were born on the earth. God knows everything about your life. He knows how your total life will turn out. God knows the number of your days on the earth. The Bible tells us that God even knows the number of hairs on your head.

> But the very hairs of your head are all numbered.
> (Matthew 10:30 KJV)

This is a true statement as well. You can count the seeds in an apple, but only God can count the apples in a seed. God is all knowing and all wise, and He is smarter than the people whom He created. When God made you, He knew exactly the way your life would turn out, including every choice you would make before you made it. God completed your life before it started on the earth. When you made Jesus your choice, your life became complete.

> And you are in Him, made full and having come to fullness of life [in Christ you too are filled with the Godhead—Father, Son and Holy Spirit—and reach full spiritual stature]. And He is the Head of all rule and authority [of every angelic principality and power].
> (Colossians 2:10 AMP)

God has already prearranged your life for good success. That being the case, why are there so many Christian not experiencing this life that God has prearranged for them to live? Have you ever had the thought enter your mind, "There has to be more to life than what I am experiencing?" Or "Why am I here?" Or "What is my purpose in life?"

We all have these types of important questions come across our minds, but the problem is this; many people do not find the answers during their lifetime. There are so many distractions keeping us from understanding the most important matters in life.

As a young boy growing up in Jackson, Mississippi, I can remember how I wanted to be a professional basketball player. My friends and I would go out in the back yard of my parents' house and play all day during the summer months, especially on Saturday. My dad and mom talked to me about being a doctor or lawyer because they felt like I could have a better life in either one of those professions.

There was nothing wrong with those professionals or my desire to play in the NBA league, to have a good job, or to make good money. It was important to me to be a good, productive citizen and provider in life. We should have that desire in our hearts to be successful and productive. Just like any good parent who wants a *good life* for his children. God's desire and will is the same for His children!

The nature of God is good! God is good to all people. The Bible says that God has his children on His mind. When you think about the goodness of God, we have so much to be thankful for: He gave us His very best by giving His Son the Lord Jesus Christ to pay the penalty for our sins, in order to bring us back into a relationship with Him, a relationship that had previously been damaged by Adam's wrong decision to disobey God.

God is a loving Father, and He has chosen to forgive all of our sins. He chose to forget and remove our sins from His mind and conscience. We all have done something wrong in our lives before, and we also know other people or our own children who have done something wrong. Should we hold that wrong against them or continue to keep that wrong before them and never forget that wrong?

If you choose to have that type of mindset, it could keep you from seeing that person for who he or she really is or keep them from the potential to be or become who God wants them to be. God knows that even when we make mistakes, if we will continue to trust Him, we will still reach the destiny that He has prepared for us. We can have the life that He has prearranged for us, the *good life*!

> For we are God s [own] handiwork (His workmanship), recreated in Christ Jesus, [born anew] that we may do those good works which God predestined (planned beforehand) for us [taking paths which He prepared ahead of time], that we should walk in them [living the *good life* which He prearranged and made ready for us to live].
> (EPHESIANS 2:10 AMP)

Why are there so many Christian not experiencing the *good life* that God has already prepared for them? Now let us look into the Word of God and find the answers!

∾ Chapter Two ∾

Why Are Some Christians Not Living the Good Life?

*The earth is the Lord's and the fullness thereof;
the world, and they that dwell therein.*
Psalm 24:1 KJV

I would like to share the main weapon that the enemy uses against the children of God. That weapon is Fear!

Growing up we are faced with so many fears. The fear of failure, rejection, acceptance, death, not having a good education, losing a relative, a relationship going bad, losing a job, or losing a home or vehicle. There are so many things in life that can cause fear to come into our lives.

Once we allow fear to come into our lives, it shatters our confidence in God and our confidence to have a successful life. Fear of failure does not come from God; it comes from the enemy of God, which is also our enemy.

When I was growing up, I had a fear of flying on an airplane. I was told, "If God wanted you to fly, He would have given you wings." In other words they were saying, "You had better stay on the ground; it's safer there."

Another fear was being afraid of the people who had expired on earth coming back to visit me in the dark. I was told so many ghost stories, which paralyzed my confidence, until I was born again and found out the truth in the Word of God.

There are many people today who have hidden and deep rooted fears that have to be removed from their spirits and minds. Fear is the greatest spiritual force that the enemy uses to attack the children of God. The devil knows that it takes faith in God for you to please God.

Faith is simply trusting God with your life and living according to His Word and according to His way. Without faith or trusting God, you cannot please Him. You must believe that He is God and that you are constantly looking to Him and depending on Him to reward you because you TRUST HIM!

Many people today are not living the *good life* because they refused to honor God by not living according to the written Word of God. They allow ungodly fear to dominate their lives. Those who love God will keep His commandments. There are so many people on earth who are in violation of the Word of God. The following are some of the violations:

1. People rejecting God.

2. People living a lifestyle that is not pleasing to God.

3. People who do not pray according to the Word of God, nor are they led by the Spirit of God.

4. People being unfaithful to The Lord.

5. People who do not support the local church with Tithes and Offerings.

6. People who are negative talkers and negative listeners.

7. People who do not have faith in God.

8. People who dishonor God appointed Authority in the home, church, government, employment, and in society.

9. People who will not study the Word of God.

10. People who do not live by the Word of Faith.

The results are not good if you chose to violate the Word of God. When people choose to live a life rejecting God, their lives becomes hard.

Some people believe that just having a lot of money makes them successful. There are a lot of people who have a lot of money who are very unhappy because they don't have a relationship with God. They are disconnected from God, so they replace God in their lives by making money their god. They know that there is a void in their lives, but instead of receiving Jesus, they live prideful lives in opposition to God.

Remember the devil's job description is threefold; to steal, to kill, and to destroy (JOHN 10:10A). He wants to conceal or steal the *good life* that God has prearranged for His people to have.

Remember Jesus was led by the Spirit of God into the wilderness to be tempted by the devil. The devil offered Jesus the kingdoms of this world by telling Jesus if He would bow down and worship him, he would give Him the kingdoms of this world. Jesus said, "It is written you shall worship the Lord God and Him only you shall serve."
(MATTHEW 4:9, 10).

Remember the devil stole Adam's authority and dominion on the earth through Adam's disobedience toward God. Jesus, the Son of God, was not going to let the devil get Him to disobey His Father God. Jesus came to destroy the works of the devil (1 JOHN 3:8). Jesus came to reconnect the people of God to God by paying the price, with His own life, for Adam's disobedience.

When you receive Jesus, your life is complete, once again. You are born again from above. Now you are reconnected with the *good life* that God has planned for you to have and live. After all, God owns everything on the earth. The earth belongs to God. The gold belongs to God. The silver belongs to God. The beasts and cattle belong to God. God also has a people who belong to Him through faith in Jesus Christ (GALATIANS 3:26).

> The earth is the Lord's and the fullness thereof; the world, and they that dwell therein.
> (PSALM 24:1 KJV)

> The silver is mine, and the gold is mine, saith the Lord of hosts.
> (HAGGAI 2:8 KJV)

For every beast of the forest is mine, and the cattle
upon a thousand hills.
(Psalm 50:10 KJV)

God has ownership of it all. We are stewards or managers here on the earth. God allows us to enjoy all of His benefits and His provisions on the earth. So don't let the devil deceive you any longer.

You need to disconnect from the devil and reconnect with God the Father right now. Make Jesus the Lord of your life. This *good life* is for you. Don't allow fear to continue to control your life keeping you separated from God.

For God hath not given us the spirit of fear; but of
power, and of love, and of a sound mind.
(2 Timothy 1:7 KJV)

In 2 Timothy 1:7, we see the spirit of fear does not come from God; the spirit of fear is given by our enemy satan; God gives us the spirit of power, of love, and of a sound mind!

But without faith, it is impossible to please and be
satisfactory to Him. For whoever would come near
to God must [necessarily] believe that God exists and
that He is the rewarder of those who earnestly and
diligently seek Him [out].
(Hebrews 11:6 AMP)

Here is an example of the spirit of fear at work in the disciples. The devil brought a storm on the sea to attempt to kill them while Jesus was resting in the boat.

And the same day, when the evening was come, he saith unto them, Let us pass over unto the other side. And when they had sent away the multitude, they took him even as he was in the ship. And there were also with him other little ships. And there arose a great storm of wind, and the waves beat into the ship, so that it was now full. And he was in the hinder part of the ship, asleep on a pillow: and they awake him, and say unto him, Master, carest thou not that we perish? And he arose, and rebuked the wind, and said unto the sea, Peace, be still. And the wind ceased, and there was a great calm. And he said unto them, Why are ye so fearful? How is it that ye have no faith? And they feared exceedingly, and said one to another, What manner of man is this, that even the wind and the sea obey him?
(Mark 4:35-41 KJV)

Fear is saying that God's Word won't work for you. Fear will stop your faith from working for you. Fear is perverted faith, and ungodly fear is doubting the Word of God. Jesus expected the disciples to use their faith to calm the storm. Instead, they forgot what He said, "Let us go over unto the other side."

The enemy will bring storms your way. That's when you need to know how to use your faith, which the Father has put in your heart. A large number of God's children are fearful when faced with opposition. Opposition is a tactic used by the enemy to keep you from living the *good life* that God has prearranged for His children.

> So don't lose your confidence. It will bring you a great reward.
> (Hebrews 10:35 GWT)

> But without faith it is impossible to please him: for he that cometh to God must believe that he is, and that he is a rewarder of them that diligently seek him.
> (Hebrews 11:6 KJV)

~: Chapter Three :~

Unforgiveness Is a Major Hindrance to The Good Life

For if ye forgive men their trespasses, your heavenly Father will also forgive you.
Matthew 6:14 KJV

Another weapon that the enemy uses is Unforgiveness! He knows that you cannot please God when you have unforgiveness, bitterness, resentment, envy, and hatred in your heart. So satan brings persecution your way to attempt to get you to walk in carnality (fleshly thinking which opposes the Word of God). The enemy does not want you to renew your mind. He wants to keep you ignorant to the knowledge and will of God for your life.

No matter what someone has done to wrong you, you must forgive them. Don't let your past mistakes, sins, failures, and disappointments keep you from reaching your destiny that God has prearranged for you: the *good life*.

I can give you many accounts in my own life when I was mistreated by a number of people on more than one occasion. I can remember times in the past when I suffered hurts. In my mind, I had good reasons to be upset and hurt, but I chose to do the right thing, which was to forgive and not try to get even or pay them back by doing something wrong. It wasn't always easy, but I made a decision to honor God's Word.

Not forgiving a person is like drinking poison. You hurt yourself in the process of trying to hurt that person. When you choose not to forgive people who have wronged you, you give them power and control over your life. When you forgive other people who have done you an injustice, you do them and yourself a favor. After all God has forgiven you of all your wrong doing!

> For if ye forgive men their trespasses, your heavenly Father will also forgive you: [15] But if ye forgive not men their trespasses, neither will your Father forgive your trespasses.
> (MATTHEW 6:14-15 KJV)

> Forbearing one another, and forgiving one another, if any man has a quarrel against any: even as Christ forgave you, so also do ye.
> (COLOSSIANS 3:13 KJV)

The enemy knows that unforgiveness will hinder your faith from working. When your faith is shipwrecked, the *good life*, God has for you will be hindered as well. As we read below in LUKE 17:3-6, Jesus teaches the disciples that forgiving your brother is the right thing to do all the time. For your faith to work, you cannot have unforgiveness in your heart.

> Take heed to yourselves: If thy brother trespass against thee, rebuke him; and if he repent, forgive him. And if he trespass against thee seven times in a day, and seven times in a day turn again to thee, saying, I repent; thou shalt forgive him. And the apostles said unto the Lord, Increase our faith. And the Lord said, If ye had faith as a grain of mustard seed, ye might say unto this sycamine tree, Be thou plucked up by the root, and be thou planted in the sea; and it should obey you.
> (LUKE 17:3-6 KJV)

> And Jesus answering saith unto them, Have faith in God. [23] For verily I say unto you, That whosoever shall say unto this mountain, Be thou removed, and be thou cast into the sea; and shall not doubt in his heart, but shall believe that those things which he saith shall come to pass; he shall have whatsoever he saith. [24] Therefore I say unto you, What things soever ye desire, when ye pray, believe that ye receive them, and ye shall have them. [25] And when ye stand praying, forgive, if ye have ought against any: that your Father also which is in heaven may forgive you your trespasses. [26] But if ye do not forgive, neither will your Father which is in heaven forgive your trespasses.
> (MARK 11:22-26 KJV)

∴ Chapter Four ∵

Rejecting God's Knowledge Will Cause Destruction in Your Life

There is an evil which I have seen under the sun, as an error which proceedeth from the ruler: Folly is set in great dignity, and the rich sit in low place. I have seen servants upon horses, and princes walking as servants upon the earth.
Ecclesiastes 10:5-7 KJV

Have you ever looked at life and seen things that seemed out of place? That the wrong people were in the right places, and the right people were in the wrong places as it pertained to the right standard of living?

The enemy will do his best to keep you in the wrong position in life. He doesn't want you to know and find your rightful place in life or in society. When you take your rightful place, then you will have a sphere of influence in the kingdom of God and in society. We as Christian should be on display for other people, letting them know how good God is and that He has a wonderful life for them. That life is called the *good life*!

Not knowing the will of God for your life and a lack of God's knowledge will keep you from reaching your destiny. The *good life* that God has prearranged for you to walk in comes by knowing and accepting His will for your life, agreeing with Him, and walking by faith in the Word of God.

> My people are destroyed for lack of knowledge: because thou hast rejected knowledge, I will also reject thee, that thou shalt be no priest to me: seeing thou hast forgotten the law of thy God, I will also forget thy children.
> (HOSEA 4:6 KJV)

> Can two walk together, except they be agreed?
> (AMOS 3:3 KJV)

We as children of God must agree with God's Word and obey Him. The Bible says that our words have power to create death or life, meaning that we can speak destruction or life to situations that we encounter. We can no longer continue to err in our talk, lack of knowledge, or our rightful position in life. Could it be that the enemy wants us to continue in our lack of knowledge so he can steal our rightful place as children of God?

> Death and life are in the power of the tongue: and they that love it shall eat the fruit thereof.
> (PROVERBS 18:21 KJV)

The children of God must walk in the light of the Word of God, in the knowledge of God. The enemy does not want you to read, study, or mediate on the Word of God. The enemy knows that the Bible is the written will of God, written by Holy men of God as the Holy Spirit inspired them. The will of God is to be passed down to the children of God throughout each generation.

> We have also a more sure word of prophecy; whereunto ye do well that ye take heed, as unto a light that shineth in a dark place, until the day dawn, and the daystar arise in your hearts: Knowing this first, that no prophecy of the scripture is of any private interpretation. For the prophecy came not in old time by the will of man: but holy men of God spake as they were moved by the Holy Ghost.
> (2 Peter 1:19-21 KJV)

> Study and be eager and do your utmost to present yourself to God approved (tested by trial), a workman who has no cause to be ashamed, correctly analyzing and accurately dividing [rightly handling and skillfully teaching] the Word of Truth.
> (2 Timothy 2:15 AMP)

> This Book of the Law shall not depart out of your mouth, but you shall meditate on it day and night, that you may observe and do according to all that is written in it. For then you shall make your way prosperous, and then you shall deal wisely and have good success.
> (Joshua 1:8 AMP)

∾ Chapter Five ∾

Don't Let Your Past Keep You from the Good Life

Bless the Lord, O my soul: and all that is within me, bless his holy name. Bless the Lord, O my soul, and forget not all his benefits.
Psalm 103:1-2 KJV

WHO FORGIVETH ALL THINE INIQUITIES; who healeth all thy diseases; Who redeemeth thy life from destruction; who crowneth thee with loving kindness and tender mercies; He hath not dealt with us after our sins; nor rewarded us according to our iniquities. For as the heaven is high above the earth, so great is his mercy toward them that fear him. As far as the east is from the west, so far hath he removed our transgressions from us. (PSALM 103:3-4, 10-12 KJV)

We as Christians sometimes have a problem with bad decisions or past hurts that hold us in bondage. We somehow believe God our Father is punishing us. The devil tells us that God is punishing you for your wrongdoing. Sometimes we believe the devil's lies and blame God for our misfortune, but all the time satan is the one condemning you.

Now don't misunderstand me; God does discipline and correct us. The Holy Spirit will convict us of our wrongdoing and show us the way out of sin. Fortunately, God put all of our sins upon Jesus. God has forgiven you for all of your sins and has removed your sins away from His memory. In other words, God has forgotten about your sins.

God is not blessing you based on what you have done or on your own abilities and works. Praise God! Your Father God is blessing you on what Jesus has already done for you. Child of God, don't ever let the devil sell you the lie that His blessing is based on your works.

The Bible says that the devil is the father of lies.

> He was a murderer from the beginning, and abode not in the truth, because there is no truth in him. When he speaketh a lie, he speaketh of his own: for he is a liar, and the father of it.
> (JOHN 8:44B KJV)

Many of God's children believe that God puts sickness upon them to teach them a lesson. Some people think God is going around killing people because they made Him angry. The truth is, God allowed His wrath and anger to be poured out upon Jesus. God is no longer angry with His children. When Jesus said that it is finished, He settled the debt in full with God for His children. The following is a list of some of the benefits that you and I receive because Jesus settled our debts with God.

THE BENEFITS:

1. God has forgiven all of your sins.

2. God has already healed you from any kind of disease or sickness.

3. God has brought or restored your life back from destruction and failure.

4. God has crowned you with His love, His kindness, His Mercy.

5. God has not dealt with you based on your sins.

6. God has not rewarded or paid you according to your sins towards Him.

7. God has decided to extend His mercy upon you forever.

8. God has decided to remove your wrongdoing as if you had never sinned.

Praise God! Sounds like a great benefit plan to me. I will take that plan any day and every day.

And you are in Him, made full and having come to fullness of life [in Christ, you too are filled with the Godhead—Father, Son, and Holy Spirit—and reach full spiritual stature]. And He is the Head of all rule and authority, of every angelic principality and power. In Him, also you were circumcised with a circumcision not made with hands, but in a [spiritual] circumcision [performed by] Christ by stripping off the body of the flesh (the whole corrupt, carnal nature with its passions and lusts). [Thus you were circumcised when] you were buried with Him in [your] bap-

tism, in which you were also raised with Him [to a new life] through [your] faith in the working of God [as displayed] when He raised Him up from the dead. And you who were dead in trespasses and in the uncircumcision of your flesh (your sensuality, your sinful carnal nature), [God] brought to life together with [Christ], having [freely] forgiven us all our transgressions, Having cancelled and blotted out and wiped away the handwriting of the note (bond) with its legal decrees and demands which was in force and stood against us (hostile to us). This [note with its regulations, decrees, and demands] He set aside and cleared completely out of our way by nailing it to [His] cross. [God] disarmed the principalities and powers that were ranged against us and made a bold display and public example of them, in triumphing over them in Him and in it [the cross].
(COLOSSIANS 2:10-15 AMP)

Praise God all my sins have been forgiven, and my slate wiped clean! Glory be to God! God does not remember your sins, so stop letting the enemy sell you this lie.

Then said Jesus to those Jews which believed on him, If ye continue in my word, then are ye my disciples indeed; And ye shall know the truth, and the truth shall make you free.
(JOHN 8:31, 32 KJV)

So Jesus said to those Jews who had believed in Him, If you abide in My word [hold fast to My teachings and live in accordance with them], you are truly My disciples. And you will know the Truth, and the Truth will set you free.
(John 8:31, 32 AMP)

Remember ye not the former things, neither consider the things of old. Behold, I will do a new thing; now it shall spring forth; shall ye not know it? I will even make a way in the wilderness, and rivers in the desert.
(Isaiah 43:18, 19 KJV)

Therefore if any person is [ingrafted] in Christ (the Messiah) he is a new creation (a new creature altogether); the old [previous moral and spiritual condition] has passed away. Behold, the fresh and new has come!
(2 Corinthians 5:17 AMP)

God has removed your old sins from your old nature out of His thought and mind. Jesus said that you shall know the truth, and the truth will make you free. The truth is that you are free from satan's powers.

~: Chapter Six :~
To Live the Good *Life* You Must Renew Your Mind

For as he thinketh in his heart, so is he.
Proverbs 23:7a KJV

You are what you think. Your faith will never go beyond what you think and believe. If your thinking is wrong, your believing will be wrong, and your speech will be wrong. You must renew your mind to line up with the Word of God. Our thoughts must be in line with His thoughts. This alignment can happen only by you having the mind of Christ.

> Seek the Lord while he may be found. Call on him while he is near. Let wicked people abandon their ways. Let evil people abandon their thoughts. Let them return to the Lord, and he will show compassion to them. Let them return to our God, because he will freely forgive them. My thoughts are not your thoughts, and my ways are not your ways, declares the Lord. Just as the heavens are higher than the earth, so my ways are higher than your ways, and my thoughts are higher than your thoughts.
> (Isaiah 55:6-9 GW)

We as Christians must renew our mind to the will of God. His Word is His will and His way. To renew our minds, we must not believe, think, talk, and conduct our life in such a way to dishonor God. The Bible teaches us that apart from Jesus we can do nothing.

> I am the vine, ye are the branches: He that abideth in me, and I in him, the same bringeth forth much fruit: for without me ye can do nothing.
> (John 15:5 KJV)

We cannot allow our lives to become disconnected from the life source, which is Jesus. We must allow our minds to be reprogrammed by the Word of God. The old mindset has to go, and the new mindset has to come for you to know the good, acceptable, and perfect will of God for your life.

Insanity is the belief that you can expect a different or better result by continuing to use the same methods or doing the same things without making any changes. Let's think about a computer's hard drive. The only thing that can be read, analyzed, or printed from the screen is the data contained on the hard drive. If you want something new to work on your computer's hard drive, you have to install a new program. The same is true with God's Word. Once you download the Word of God to your mind, it remains, and you are set for eternity.

> I beseech you therefore, brethren, by the mercies of God, that ye present your bodies a living sacrifice, holy, acceptable unto God, which is your reasonable service. [2] And be not conformed to this world: but be ye transformed by the renewing of your mind,

that ye may prove what is that good, and acceptable, and perfect, will of God.
(Romans 12:1-2 KJV)

The Bible says that we have the mind of Christ. We need to see ourselves the way our Heavenly Father sees us!

> For who has known or understood the mind (the counsels and purposes) of the Lord so as to guide and instruct Him and give Him knowledge? But we have the mind of Christ (the Messiah) and do hold the thoughts (feelings and purposes) of His heart.
> (1 Corinthians 2:16 AMP)

∽ Chapter Seven ∾

God's Blessing and Favor Empowers You to Be Successful

*God's blessing makes life rich;
nothing we do can improve on God.*
Proverbs 10:22 MSG

THE BLESSING IS AN EMPOWERMENT to live the *good life*. When the blessing is working in your life, you will excel in the *good life*, and experience increase and abundance in every area of your life. Instead of sickness, you will have good health, instead of poverty, you will have abundant wealth and, instead of confusion, you will have peace. The Apostle John said, "Beloved, I pray that you may prosper in every way and [that your body] may keep well, even as [I know] your soul keeps well and prospers." (3 John 1:2 AMP)

> BLESSED (HAPPY, fortunate, prosperous, and enviable) is the man who walks and lives not in the counsel of the ungodly [following their advice, their plans

and purposes], nor stands [submissive and inactive] in the path where sinners walk, nor sits down [to relax and rest] where the scornful [and the mockers] gather. But his delight and desire are in the law of the Lord, and on His law (the precepts, the instructions, the teachings of God) he habitually meditates (ponders and studies) by day and by night. And he shall be like a tree firmly planted [and tended] by the streams of water, ready to bring forth its fruit in its season; its leaf also shall not fade or wither; and everything he does shall prosper [and come to maturity].
(PSALM 1:1-3 AMP)

The blessed man according to the Word of God is:

1. A happy man.

2. A fortunate man.

3. A prosperous man.

4. A man who does not follow ungodly advice from people.

5. A man who chooses to live a life that pleases God.

6. A man who takes delight and desire in studying and thinking on the Word of God.

A blessed man will be firmly planted in the ways of the Lord, and He will become successful in life God's way. The Word of God also talks about the *Favor of God* that is upon the righteous people's life. Favor is God taking delight in you; it is God's acceptance and approval of your life. It is God being good to you. When you honor the Lord with your life, God's provision, protection, peace, and preferential treatment become a part of your life.

> For thou, Lord, wilt bless the righteous; with favour wilt thou compass him as with a shield.
> (PSALM 5:12 KJV)

God will always bless righteous people, who were made right with Him through the life of Jesus. The bible says that Jesus knew no sin, but was made to be sin for us, that we would be made the righteous of God in Christ.

> Let them shout for joy, and be glad, that favour my righteous cause: yea, let them say continually, Let the Lord be magnified, which hath pleasure in the prosperity of his servant.
> (PSALM 35:27 KJV)

In the above scripture, the psalmist David teaches us the importance of shouting for joy, being glad, and making God big in our life. God will favor righteous people and He takes great delight in their prosperity. We are God's righteous people and His desire is to see us walking in prosperity.

> My son, do not forget my teachings, and keep my commands in mind, because they will bring you long life, good years, and peace. Do not let mercy and truth leave you. Fasten them around your neck. Write them on the tablet of your heart. Then you will find favor

and much success in the sight of God and humanity. Trust the Lord with all your heart, and do not rely on your own understanding. In all your ways acknowledge him, and he will make your paths smooth. Do not consider yourself wise. Fear the Lord, and turn away from evil. Then your body will be healed, and your bones will have nourishment. Honor the Lord with your wealth and with the first and best part of all your income. Then your barns will be full, and your vats will overflow with fresh wine.
(Proverbs 3:1-10 GWT)

But remember the Lord your God is the one who makes you wealthy. He is confirming the promise which he swore to your ancestors. It's still in effect today.
(Deuteronomy 8:18 GWT)

God has not changed His mind about you living the *good life*. God's plan for His children remains the same. The bible says that God cannot lie, and that Jesus is the same yesterday, today, and forever. The Lord is ready to bless His people.

Thou shalt arise, and have mercy upon Zion: for the time to favour her, yea, the set time, is come.
(Psalm 102:13 KJV)

Zion refers to the people of God. The bible teaches us that to everything, there is a season. It is our season; it is our time to live the *good life*.

Chapter Eight

It Is Our Time to Shine

Arise, shine; for thy light is come,
and the glory of the Lord is risen upon thee.
Isaiah 60:1 KJV

The Lord spoke to me on December 18, 2011, concerning His Children. The Lord spoke to my spirit and said, "Now is the time for my children to rise and shine."

> Arise [from the depression and prostration in which circumstances have kept you—rise to a new life]! Shine (be radiant with the glory of the Lord), for your light has come, and the glory of the Lord has risen upon you!
> (Isaiah 60:1 AMP)

To arise is to come to a new or different position in your spirit, soul, and body. Your entire life should be operating on a higher level according to the Word of God. When you receive revelation from the Word of God, you see and experience what others do not see and understand.

I believe that the Sons of God are beginning to manifest on the earth today. I believe the church is getting ready to enter its finest hour. To live the *good life*, you must know who you are in Christ; you must come to grips with your true identity.

The Word of God says in Psalm chapter eight, "What is man?" Do you really know who you are? There are so many of God's children who are living beneath the will of God for their own personal lives. The Word of God teaches us that the will of God is for His children to have good health and to live a prosperous life. The Word of God is medicine to all of our human body. The Word will help strengthen our spirits, souls, and bodies!

The Bible teaches us that as a man thinks, so is he. As long as we have the wrong image of God and ourselves, we will live a life of shame and defeat. This condition is not the will of God! The Word of God says that the God in us is greater than the god in the people who don't have a relationship with God. We as children of God should be living a life that is victorious.

The Bible declares that God doesn't keep any good thing away from His children. We as children of God must not allow the enemy to steal our joy and peace of the Lord. The joy of The Lord is our strength, and the peace of God is what gives us victory over the enemy in every area of our life. When you keep your heart and mind stayed upon Jesus, your peace becomes perfected peace, meaning that it will keep you strong during the storms of life. Peace will calm your storms in life.

As children of God, we need to take a stand on the written Word of God, to submit to God, and resist the devil in our lives. Then the devil will flee from us. When satan brings temptations, sickness, diseases, confusion, or strife, your way

God has already given you a way out. Faith in His Word is your way out of any problem you may encounter with satan and allows you to live the *good life*.

> There isn't any temptation that you have experienced which is unusual for humans. God, who faithfully keeps his promises, will not allow you to be tempted beyond your power to resist. But when you are tempted, he will also give you the ability to endure the temptation as your way of escape.
> (1 Corinthians 10:13 GWT)

> That it might be fulfilled which was spoken by Esaias the prophet, saying, Himself took our infirmities, and bare our sicknesses.
> (Matthew 8:17 KJV)

> Who his own self bare our sins in his own body on the tree, that we, being dead to sins, should live unto righteousness: by whose stripes ye were healed.
> (1 Peter 2:24 KJV)

> Christ hath redeemed us from the curse of the law, being made a curse for us: for it is written, Cursed is every one that hangeth on a tree: That the blessing of Abraham might come on the Gentiles through Jesus Christ; that we might receive the promise of the Spirit through faith. And if ye be Christ's, then are ye Abraham's seed, and heirs according to the promise.
> (Galatians 3:13, 14, 29 KJV)

Jesus paid the price for all of our sins, weakness, sickness, confusion, and poverty. Jesus paid the price for all of our punishment from God, so that we could live a life free from the power of sin, weakness, sickness, confusion, and poverty. It is called the *good life*.

When God created the first family on the earth, they lived in perfect harmony with God. There was no lack of provision, no sickness in their bodies, they had a good marriage, a great job, and God came to visit them every day. God prearranged this life for all His children to live with Him. The same life Adam and Eve had in the Garden of Eden before they disobeyed God. That plan has never changed; it is still in place for His children today.

God's desire is to bless the marriage between a man and a woman. God intended for Adam and Eve to live the *good life* and He intends for us to live the *good life*.

> And the Lord God caused a deep sleep to fall upon Adam, and he slept: and he took one of his ribs, and closed up the flesh instead thereof; And the rib, which the Lord God had taken from man, made he a woman, and brought her unto the man. And Adam said, This is now bone of my bones, and flesh of my flesh: she shall be called Woman, because she was taken out of Man. Therefore shall a man leave his father and his mother, and shall cleave unto his wife: and they shall be one flesh. And they were both naked, the man and his wife, and were not ashamed.
>
> (Genesis 2:21-25 KJV)

Whoso findeth a wife findeth a good thing,
and obtaineth favour of the Lord.
(Proverbs 18:22 KJV)

We know that the Word of God gives us a firm foundation to build upon. When God made man, He made man without any defects. He did not have to do a recall on His creation! God made you very special and unique.

What is man, that thou art mindful of him? and the son of man, that thou visitest him? For thou hast made him a little lower than the angels, and hast crowned him with glory and honour. Thou madest him to have dominion over the works of thy hands; thou hast put all things under his feet.
(Psalm 8:4-6 KJV)

The Greek noun for angels in this passage of scripture is Elohim, meaning God or the true God. You are made in His Image and likeness. You are somebody; you are the highest of all of God's creation. Stop saying that you are a nobody. Stop saying that you will never amount to anything. Stop saying that you will never be anything. Start saying what God says about you. Start seeing yourself the way God sees you!

For thou has made him a little lower than the angels,
and hast crowned him with glory and honor.
(Psalm 8:5 KJV)

Man has been crowned with glory and honor! Angels are not crowned with glory and honor; they are ministering spirits sent forth to minister for those who are heirs of salvation.

> But to which of the angels said he at any time, Sit on my right hand, until I make thine enemies thy footstool? Are they not all ministering spirits, sent forth to minister for them who shall be heirs of salvation?
> (Hebrews 1:13, 14 KJV)

In the passage above, are the Angels not ALL ministering spirits called to serve? According to this meaning, man is a little bit lower than God Himself. That means that we are in a class above the angelic class of being. After all, the Bible says in the book of Genesis, that God made us in His image and likeness. I know the Creator is above the creation; God is above the angels, so we are in a God class below Almighty God!

> And God said, Let us make man in our image, after our likeness: and let them have dominion over the fish of the sea, and over the fowl of the air, and over the cattle, and over all the earth, and over every creeping thing that creepeth upon the earth. So God created man in his own image, in the image of God created he him; male and female created he them. And God blessed them, and God said unto them, Be fruitful, and multiply, and replenish the earth, and subdue it: and have dominion over the fish of the sea, and over the fowl of the air, and over every living thing that moveth upon the earth.
> (Genesis 1:26-28 KJV)

All of Creation is waiting on the sons of God to live the *good life* that God has pre-arranged for them. Are you ready to Rise and Shine in Jesus; the LIGHT has COME!

> [But what of that?] For I consider that the sufferings of this present time (this present life) are not worth being compared with the glory that is about to be revealed to us and in us and for us and conferred on us! For [even the whole] creation (all nature) waits expectantly and longs earnestly for God s sons to be made known [waits for the revealing, the disclosing of their sonship].
> (ROMANS 8:18, 19 AMP)

Now you know why the enemy is afraid of you living the *good life*, for it brings glory to God. So let your light shine before all men, glorifying your Father God in Heaven.

> For I know the thoughts and plans that I have for you, says the Lord, thoughts and plans for welfare and peace and not for evil, to give you hope in your final outcome.
> (JEREMIAH 29:11 AMP)

> For we are God s [own] handiwork (His workmanship), recreated in Christ Jesus, [born anew] that we may do those good works which God predestined (planned beforehand) for us [taking paths which He prepared ahead of time], that we should walk in them [living the *good life* which He prearranged and made ready for us to live].
> (EPHESIANS 2:10 AMP)

I believe the dreams and visions that God has given you before have been resurrected in your life. I believe your understanding about your Father God has been settled forever. God is good all of the time. Jesus is the same yesterday, today, and forever.

I trust this book has been a blessing to you. Every time I read through the pages, I receive more revelation from The Lord. I pray that the Lord has opened your heart, your mind, and your eyes. I thank the Spirit of God for leading you to read this book, for you did not read this book by accident. So I thank you for purchasing the book.

I speak blessing over your life in Jesus Name. May the Lord cause His Face to shine upon you, with long life and good days ahead and may the blessings of the Lord overtake you. Right now, you are the blessed of the Lord!

Praise the Lord I am living the GOOD LIFE!
Columbus O'Banner Jr.

Prayer of Salvation

*For all have sinned, and come
short of the glory of God.*
Romans 3:23 KJV

For God so loved the world, that he gave his only begotten Son, that whosoever believeth in him should not perish, but have everlasting life. (John 3:16 KJV)

But what saith it? The word is nigh thee, even in thy mouth, and in thy heart: that is, the word of faith, which we preach; That if thou shalt confess with thy mouth the Lord Jesus, and shalt believe in thine heart that God hath raised him from the dead, thou shalt be saved. For with the heart man believeth unto righteousness; and with the mouth confession is made unto salvation. For the scripture saith, Whosoever believeth on him shall not be ashamed. For there is no difference between the Jew and the Greek: for the same Lord over all is rich unto all that call upon him. For whosoever shall call upon the name of the Lord shall be saved.
(Romans 10:8-13 KJV)

God loves you regardless of your life. God sent His son Jesus to die on the cross for every person born into this world. Jesus died and rose again for our justification. If you would like to receive Jesus into your life, please pray this prayer sincerely from your heart; confessing with your mouth:

> Heavenly Father, I come to you right now admitting that I am a sinner. I believe that Jesus died on the cross for my sins and that He rose again from the dead on the third day. Lord Jesus, I ask you to come into my heart by faith right now and make me a new creature in Christ Jesus. Now, Father, according to your Word if I believe in my heart and confess with my mouth that God raised Jesus from the dead, I shall be saved. I believe with all of my heart, Father, that you raised Jesus from the dead, and He is my Lord. Now, thank you Father for saving me by grace though faith in Jesus name. Amen.

If you prayed this prayer to receive Jesus as your savior and Lord, please write us to receive more information about your new life in Christ.

Columbus O'Banner Ministries
P.O. Box 824
Magee, MS 39111

About the Author

Now the just shall live by faith.
Hebrews 10:38a KJV

Pastor Columbus O'Banner Jr. is a native of Jackson, Mississippi. He and his loving wife Barbara currently reside in Byram, MS. Together they have four children and six grandchildren. They serve as pastors at Mt. Moriah Church located in Magee, MS. where they believe "Now the Just Shall Live by Faith."

Pastor O'Banner Jr. is the founder and CEO of Columbus O'Banner Ministries. He accepted Christ into his life on August 3, 1977. The following year on February 2, 1978, he received the baptism in the Holy Spirit. In June of 1978, he accepted the call into the ministry. Pastor O'Banner Jr. presently serves under the leadership of Senior Pastor Joel Sims of Word of Life Church, located in Flowood, MS.

Pastor O'Banner Jr. and his wife are graduates of Word of Life Bible Training Center and ordained ministers of Word of Life Ministerial Association. They are also members of Creflo Dollar Ministerial Association (CDMA), founded by Dr. Creflo A. Dollar and Fellowship of International Christian Word of Faith Ministries (FICWFM), founded by Apostle Dr. Frederick K.C. Price.

Pastor O'Banner Jr. and his wife have a heart's desire to see the body of Christ united and flowing together in unity, love, faith, peace, and power. They believe, as pastors, they must edify and equip the believers to do the work of the ministry and make full proof of the ministry. Knowing that when believers do the work of the ministry, they will see the power, glory, blessing, and miracles return to the body of Christ.

The Bible says that there is One Lord, One Faith, One Baptism (Eph 4:5 AMP). God has called us to be a people of honor and excellence and to operate in Divine Order. Columbus O'Banner Ministries places their emphasis on teaching the uncompromising Word of Faith.

www.ingramcontent.com/pod-product-compliance
Lightning Source LLC
Chambersburg PA
CBHW071757040426
42446CB00012B/2603